Rendition for
Harp & Kalashnikov

By the same author:

Poetry
The Pallbearer's Garden
The Wind-up Birdman of Moorabool Street

Novel
Eugene's Falls

Nonfiction
Australian Fiction as Archival Salvage

Rendition for
Harp & Kalashnikov

A. Frances Johnson

PUNCHER & WATTMANN

First published in 2017
Published by Puncher and Wattmann
PO Box 441
Glebe NSW 2037

http://www.puncherandwattmann.com

puncherandwattmann@bigpond.com

National Library of Australia
Cataloguing-in-Publication entry:

Johnson, A. Frances

Rendition for Harp & Kalashnikov

ISBN   9781922186966

I. Title.

A821.3

Cover design by Sophie Gaur

Printed by Lightning Source International

This project has been assisted by the Australian Government through the Australia Council, its arts funding and advisory body.

Australian Government

Australia | Council
for the Arts

Contents

I: Soar

II: Sore

II: Saw

i.m. Tom Johnson 1925–2014

... we didn't see our dead,
Who rarely bothered coming home to die
But simply stayed away out there
In the clean war, the war in the air.
— Howard Nemerov

My hand on the map
as if on an old scar.
— Dunya Mikhail

I: Soar

Soar

It began with structural analysis
of a dragonfly wing.
The first task: to create
flow in the DelFly II,
wing flexibility in 'clap-and-fling'
and 'clap-and-peel'. In the end
they took a sky segmentation approach;
others tested complex tail effects
in flapping flight.

Even so, after years of work,
hear-and-avoid problems beset
indoor and outdoor dragonflies.
Certain parties insisted on micro air vehicles
quieter than any insect that ever hovered
over a lake ('water source').
One bright spark solved it.

You want quiet? I'll give you guys quiet, he said.
This is gunna be the quietest bug on the planet,
quieter than anything we've done before;
quieter than any soft-spoken woman at a well
shielding her eyes from the glare,
from dreams of water
in the insectless heat of high summer.

Hummingbird

Target accuracy of poems
as with fixed-wing UAVs
varies wildly.
Only the remote operator
reads intention like a book.
This is his bastard ghazal.
Unlike the poet,
he won't discuss payload,
precise and imprecise hovering,
the true arc
of his bird's avian stunts.
That's how the poem began
and ended, looking for trajectory,
for onscreen radiance,
explosions in quiet rooms.

Tow

For, lo, the winter is past, the rain is over and gone
The flowers appear on the earth; the time of the singing of birds is come ...

Song of Solomon 2:11–12, KJV

Lo, the cell phone sleeps in its cell.
The raven deactivates the horizon.
There is water for everyone,
but not the kind you can drink.
The interdiction crews bring slabs
of plastic bottles and one-syllable words
deployed with biblical clarity:
no, tow, flow, go, foe.

Lo, watch the oil on the water
shimmer, a miracle of evidence.
Wounded rainbows
leak from under the hull. For days,
the reaper drone shadows
its nest of wood, dreaming
of the time after rain,
flowers appearing on earth,
the singing of birds,
the winter over and gone.

Fuse

Wire was once a useful thing.
Piano wire brought song,
made the piannola in the desert
unspool melodies to support
a soldier's farmblock optimism.
Wire brushes cleaned the mud
from workboots, penned animals
inside their stalls. Fine gauge
fixed the porcelain fuse

so a light globe shone
over airconditioned Bethlehem.
And here, razor wire
taught children what to expect.

Photograph

He avoids dining out
on his award-winning photograph.
Its forced correspondence nags;
he has seen this room before,
filed the same shot, the one
with the camp hall of mirrors.
He knows how the poem goes
before the poet has written it:
he will not dine out on it;
on the one of many.
But the next night he books
a restaurant, a good one,
eating past life.
When a little death
on a plate arrives, he cuts
the image away
like an army surgeon.

Love song

Bastard variations in form and song
have been known to ruin a good city.
Hummingbird drones, for example, passing the dried fruit markets
singing and looking for mates, play out 'hear and avoid' variations.
The more solid the object or wall, the louder their thrum.
When clear passage is guaranteed, the birds make almost no sound.
But consider the bee-like hum. Merchants and shoppers don't notice,
but children think how curious that a market
 should be full, suddenly, of bees.

This technological *pianissimo* is a subtle achievement.
But for scientists, flawed 'hear and avoid' mechanisms are dead giveaways.
There can be no stealth without concealment of song.
Some days a vagueness of pitch confuses the young corporal on headsets.
When his birds do not return, he can still hear them over the wire,
over the shush of white noise, mimicking the harmonics
of ancient Urdu love songs.

Birds

no longer recognise
non-segmented skies
or sing in the face of obstacles.
Overall, the sighing cloud
is less trained, less *orderly*
than the hummingbird would like.
This does not stop it moving close
to the wire, behind which
disorganised families prepare
meals of goat and bitter greens.
Radio Afghanistan is heard far distant,
the desert's soft shoe.
The bird tracks and targets.
Where necessary, it drops payload.
The young corporal on headsets listens in,
discharge, a pure lyric. *Turn it up, man!*
He and his birds are never fooled
by sugared Persian love songs.
After some days, the bird flies back,
lonely at 18kph, whirring perpetual dawn.

Unmanned aerial vehicle versus poem

The UAV hunts the sword
until sand settles
the blade.

The poem, once unmanned,
also performs delicate feats
of waypoint navigation.

Both crafts demonstrate mixed flight
behaviours, their trajectories
monitored by others.

Weighing less than the smallest UAV
(at under 700 grams,
still weightier than a page),

the poem is less reliable
in open space, but more flexible
than fixed-wing models

favouring the single reading.

Soar II: String that holds the sky[1]

The bird dips and soars, unseasonally.
No string to hold it, no small boy mechanism.
It has an unobstructed view of spring terrain,
North Waziristan − rock-spattered with the bitter greens
that grow in this part of the world.
These are added to a stew of goat;
the leaves wrap staples of whey curd.
The bird is not in the business of ethnic food porn,
winged poetries, canons of flight.
Its interests: sky segmentation, target and discharge;
guided movements, shadows,
shapes that cannot be caged or catalogued.
Of vegetables, a grandmother who has known
her seasons of soaring and sadness knows a great deal.
Midwifery is her profession, okra her speciality.
She steps confidently into the field of summer
with her grandchildren, 67 years' experience
under her belt. The crop is abundant, reason to celebrate.
The sky is blue, birds soar. Momina, Momina Bibi!

Her son Rafiq, a school teacher, her first pearl, and her two
pearlers, grandchildren Zubair and Nabila,
testify at the American congressional hearing.
The concierge at the hotel insists on ironing

---

1 Rafiq ur Rehman, a Pakistani primary school teacher who appeared
on Capitol Hill with his children, Zubair, 13, and Nabila, 9, described his
mother, Momina Bibi, as the 'string that held our family together'. His two
children, gathering okra with their grandmother the day she was killed,
were injured in an attack that took place on 24 October 2012 in a tribal area
of North Waziristan. Their harrowing accounts marked the first time Congress had ever heard from civilian victims of an alleged US drone strike.

their collars, their papers. The granddaughter
steps to the microphone.
I heard the dum dum noise. This was not a bird.
She insists. *Birds are smarter than that.*
The grandson says: *I prefer cloudy days when the drones don't fly.*
When the sky brightens and becomes blue.
He points to his sister's drawing: a house, a field,
two birds, three figures, the great mountain rising up.
The son says: *In Urdu we have a saying:*
aik lari main pro kay rakhna
(the string that holds the pearls together).
The string is broken. The mountain holds,
a confusion of song.

Free quote

Our barbed wire is braided by a system of constant torsion around the line, barb prongs interlaced. Two pieces of stainless steel razor or zinc-coated razor wire are bound together by clips, sharp points arranged at intervals along the strand. Twist types include single twist, double twist, and traditional twist. *Note, these are not dance moves.* To prevent humans climbing through or over barbed wire fences, our razor wire variants feature near-continuous cutting surfaces sufficient to injure unprotected persons. *Thus, dancing cannot occur.*

Features of both kinds of wire include compact and rational structure, high safety factors, and efficacy in the protection of prisons and key security projects. Galvanised barbed wire fencing is also used for the enclosure of animals, while barbed wire fences in green PVC can be used for fencing in backyards and gardens. Care is required during installation to avoid serious hurt. *Only you must keep the key to the lock.*

Our razor wire, in galvanised or stainless steel, comes in a variety of forms, such as flat razor wire, straight type and concertina wire. *Again, 'concertina' bears no reference to music machines. The functionalities and applications of music are outside our ambit.* Our welded razor wire fence and flat razor fencing are popular products in today's world. As popular as music. If you need more information about barbed wire and concertina razor wire, please contact us now for a free quote. *We stop everything from moving towards you.*

The problem of Russian novels in the desert

My blood freezes without thermometers, *cris du coeur*, fuss. Soon it is so cold I forget to go home; no trusted servants come. From my father's old wooden chair I watch the avocets fall down dead upon the desert steppes; the weather closes in like a violent master looking to beat itself out against thin glass sunsets. Some days, I imagine I remember love. Warmth. My father's tight fist, coiled decades of harm. Other days, I think on how my own work as a tyrant kept me busy. I recall no fireside delicacies of chat; the fur-collared ineluctabilities of Russian novels. In those, fate is always tightly costumed by weather; the wit delicious. I could never convince my guard that poetry was an interest of mine. Caches of weapons arrived, but the infidels regularly forgot to pack the novels alongside. In between massacres, I wanted to call them to ask … how was it that an overcoat was invisible, like air?

But now, the readership, my readership, dies off. Snow, steam and good character do not save; 'save as' fails to uncouple deathly amities between desert and glacier. Thus, I grow still and stolid under the blasted pine, *Pinus brutia*. Yes, power is of no use! This is fate of a kind, though not a literary one. I was finally schooled to maim and defile, not monitor floods, droughts and words, the outcome of another story. The weather and its good-for-nothing king has been my great oversight. I am just alive with the bitterness of it, taunted by spite winds that ruin the blank-screened sky, mocking my clanking medals, my university-trained urge for judicious rewrites of the past. Still, I am grudgingly respectful. Elemental cruelty has no campaign, no magnificent strategy; it runs the shop by sheer force, as my late father did in his epauletted heyday. Decrees and mandates, paid-up salutations and an endless supply of Kalashnikovs mean naught. The weather is a dread Napoleon.

I, like so many others, am being frozen out in the act of being frozen. Since Thursday, Lake Assad, the Euphrates and the sea are become one; our last known words bury in green-shot ice. I still recognise the letters: Arabic, French, English. Drowned ciphers of great beauty that were once mine. But who can parse these buried glyphs? What old words spell out in glacial violet? The questions tire me, as does this strange winter. I long for comfort but the keen-nosed dog or loyal horse no longer nuzzle my palms, loping or trotting away in fear; they, too, stand frozen inside the gate of my private zoo, alongside rigid zebras and gazelles, kangaroos and jackals. No arc sails the borderless seas. Romantic heroines no longer jump in front of trains.

My lover loves but does not find me; Asma's palace roofline was the first to disappear in the vast snows. She is far away – a cloaking memory; a velvet-skinned extinction. I imagine her bitter manuscripts (memoirs all) thickening like peat in the vast gilt attic; our old medical books, all the beautiful propoganda, a blurred, spent fuel. Forget about reading, I implore you! Oblomov, Karamazov, Raskolnikov are no use any more. I now regard time with a gull's cold eye, cosying up to avian metaphors, though I can barely tell the difference between kites and drones. My blood seems poikilothermic now, much like that of the ibis, last survivor at the edge of the lake. But still I cannot fly. Expectation of transfiguration, flight, you see, remains strong. This makes me laugh, the disastrous, pretty, Christian ruin of it, oh yes, an artful foreign influence! Like Dostoevsky, I gamble everything but I cannot write off my debts. And so I mount the icy scaffold, dear friends ...

Survival is something else again. I used to be good at it. But then, I had help. Even still, in our last days the ice does not mummify completely, but preserves me half alive in its waterless lexicon, never calling me to account. At first we hid the bodies in the rivers. Naaman of old, very naturally, thought the warm rivers of Damascus, Abana and Pharpar far better than all the waters of Israel (look it up for yourselves, don't be lazy: 2 Kings 5:12). I always liked any flood that helped conceal a flood of evidence. That red river of dissent was my delight ... my enemies strung out under a Damascene sunset. Passing through to the sea. Away and away and away!

Still, my ice-cracked brain allows me one last dream before sleep: the coming of spring. The old warmth and its wisdoms! I hold the idea of it in my lap like a child. I am like Levin, returning to the straw-gathered countryside after wearying of marriage games in the salons of St Petersburg. I drop my head back for absolution. No wise mufti comes to chant a legal ghazal or two. My last vision before sleep, dear Asma, is this: the lush beauty of Syrian rivers, fringed by date palms and market gardens. People praying and laughing, feasting and dancing throughout the oldest and most beautiful, fertile settlements in the world. Homs, Aleppo, Aqrab, Deir-ez-Zor ... places gifted great libraries of time. It has taken resolve to shape out the pure, shelfless plane of palimpsest. To rise above time itself! To begin again. Oh yes! I cleave to the idea of myself as mythic, to the idea that, with the coming of the warm spring rains, I will be carried ceremoniously, like a revered Syrian queen in her sedan chair, down to the rushing river of history, even as I become its seated, bloated afterword.

Say something

1942	I don't have to be captured	to capture
1994	I don't need to fire a sniper's rifle	to snipe
1990	I don't need a service record	to write an order of service
2011	I don't need to go to war	to write of war
2008	I don't need to embed myself	to bed down the enemy
1916	I don't need to dig a trench	to be entrenched
1992	I don't need to deploy chemical weapons	to poison
1945	I don't have to sit still	to be stilled
1961	I don't have to kill	to be killed
2012	I don't have to program drones	to drone on
1969	I don't need to be discharged	to vet disinformation
2010	I don't need to suffer PTSS	to repudiate acronyms
1918	I don't need to gather poppies	to remember
2013	I don't have to die laughing	to die sober
2016	I don't need to do anything	to say something

Acquainted

I have walked through deserts and over dunes.
I have been acquainted with great heat,
outwalked the camp protection goons.

I have passed northern armies decked in green,
passed southern militia on the lam,
drunk from illusions of brook and stream.

Quiet as a gun at each new border,
I queue for my NGO-issue tent,
dreaming of my mother's patient order.

When the map moves under a tuneless moon,
I move with it, a magnet's child,
back through deserts and over dunes.

Ultima Thule: Swimming lessons

The moon is at it again. Hazarding the return
of a triumphant salt order. The cinder-block
metropolis demurs. Does not believe in anything beyond
solidity and glittering affect. They say this much is true:
all low-lying capitals will be subject to the same flood
and brought low. But I'm not interested
in biblical trickery, talk of light and dark,
swimming lessons given by creatures
I have mostly met battered and fried.
Your best stroke, what is it? Friend, you must prepare!
I walk around the office, shake hands with the many,
but not with those who can swim.
A decision has been made, but I forget by whom.
By the drinking fountain I feel immense loss;
I realise I have never much spoken with the dead.
I am so struck by this, I am effusive to the cold fish
in management. I grab her painted hand and blurt out
my thirsty wonder in sloshing oceanic tones,
Sediment in a cup may be my last hope, my Ultima Thule.
She says, *You are not yet ready for promotion.*
When the lift plummets to the new concourse,
I must remember to jump before impact.
Surviving that, I won't gloat, or reminisce how
I saw the archaeology of flood in small things.
Or confess how, for a long time, water sounded
in my ears like a shell, held close.
For now, the broken drinking fountain prevails;
symptom of the greater thirst, and the contempt
of the gathering storm. Outside, dark suits,
not yet mourners, broker deals between wavering

curtain walls. If I mimic their confidence, my risk,
even at this late stage, will become certainty. Asset.
I do my best. I try to swim in frozen oceans
of cash, brokered by stylish bankers and bardic thieves.
But I have things on my mind:
unfinished compliance, the eyeless storm, you.
Managers no longer look me in the eye —
where I am concerned, theirs is a drought affection.
I turn the sand-timer over on my blotter. *Look*, I want to say,
my gold carat heart was boiled down long ago;
yearnings for liquidity began early.
I was not easily haltered, in water or air.
As a child, I saved energy, cash, sweets … lethargically.
I did not hoard. Even after posses of grave-faced bankers
visited my school. How my brother pitied me, treading water
against the facts. Turning plain accounting into doubtful poetry.
Back then, we were presented with a saving choice:
a small porcelain pig or miniature tin bank building.
Neither pig nor pediment convinced; the closed shapes of pools
did not deceive. No-one thought on how to build a boat.
What to do when the water came.

The next day, I woke at my desk.
I had been waiting years for swimming lessons
in a city without a pool. Heavy rain beat sideways
against the curtain glass. We'd made no provisions
for oars or rafts. The sky was a rinsed violet,
riven with sulphurous cumulus, long shafts of light.
We stood by our desks in solemn commemoration
of something we'd failed to name. A great noise rose up,
as if all the insects of the world had gathered together to sing.
Glass me into this town of unbelief,
this dry hoard, it's inability to imagine the arc,

the saving of things. I was not the only one
who'd been content with 'save as'.

Now I cannot stroke my way out.

Romanticism

Back then the 'I' merged
with the ragged stream
plunging through
the paintable ravine.

Now the 'I' regales
implanted hills,
meadows of plastic,
rhymed ocean spills;

still excess.

Sea level

for Anthony Lynch

You can't see water beyond the highway hoardings, but you are told
        Jesus walked on it.
This is your best clue. Signs for dinner settings, security doors, viagra
        and tractor parts
flash past like miracles.

But you feel something pull, not daintily at your sleeve, but with tidal will,
pulling blood into stark equations of space and gravity you cannot
        hope to solve.

When you get there, sea fills out the world beyond the wildest hopes
of plumbers and drinking fountains, the dramatic imaginings of
        poets. Stop there.

The salt order threatens but that is what you wanted, that genius
        rise and fall,
its white-noised repeat; the fierce marine gull as priest, chanting
        agitprop.

Why is it that only solid things insist as civilisation?
All architectures house a vacuum, await the pourer, the pouring in.

Whether this is ocean or something molten, earth, an infil of words
        — you must decide.
Swimming against the tide won't help; new speech quickly becomes
        lack of speech.

You've learnt the lessons of containment: skyscrapers and houses,
        banks and zoos.

In the city, people press their hands against glass and feel the pulsing
            tremor of curtain walls.

You are like them; this is part and parcel of your day job, listening to
            life moving through
encryption. Knowing that, in the end, all your resolutions will melt.

On the way back from the coast you notice cavernous shops selling
            light fittings,
acres and acres of lights, a confusion of Bethlehems.

In the distance the city skyline glows with penthoused unbelief.
You shift in closer now, you have come back − strong, certain as tides.

High-altitude archaeologist

for Constanza Cerutti and Shari Kocher

They sang to her, the mountains. For a long time
she couldn't see her way to the top, this century or that.
But by 2000, she had claimed her professional stripes,
poetries of palimpsest, her dreamt vertigo.
She climbed alone, then with others.
She uttered 'my vocation',
as if she was married to God.
But she did not cut her lovely hair.
Eventually the male climbers came to admire her fortitude,
her focus. This did not stop them taking credit.
When the precious objects came off the mountain,
packed in haloes of dry ice, the child mummies'
breathed soft as a sleep sacrifice.

She did not pause for ancient recriminations.
She organised the fridges, the transports out.
She climbed up and down; they wrote her off as a nun.
The mountain sang to her, never cold.

Awesome

after Caspar David Friedrich

At what point did awe take on 'some'?
Who saw the volcano's lip invert
through the prism of a plastic shard?
High on sulphurous opiates, sheer altitude,
the trekker pauses, repudiates
scratchy Byronic notations,
replicates the stance of
the first man on the mountain
without a thought.
This rainbowed template is his!
Not another first man, the mountain sighs,
as the second man up takes the shot.

Australian awe

for Marcia Langton

The rock-art guide, combusting
in 42 degrees, back to image.
His sloppy dreamtime,
a melted ice-cream,
far from refrigerated sublime.

Some whites reckon
pre-contact was one big
happy black campout,
lasting millennia.
That's so's they can conveniently
keep Aboriginal people in some
pre-modern place.

It's a quote, I said,
as people lowered their cameras
heartwards, like Jesus
snapping a selfie.
We all want the fridge.
Country is no caravan park.
The guide wiped his brow
with a neckerchief of
ochre-tinted dots, the rest
pixellating behind him.

What's wrong with you?
What did art ever do to you?

Icarus at the all-night supply

The moon rose like it had been hit,
as if it had staggered back
from the ropes for another try.

It was one thing to hold
bruised, satin light
to pummelled night skies

where all bets were off.
Punters knew the sun
would soon take the guy

down to daylight's ropes —
the quiet field, the sleeping mall
strip-searched by dawn cries.

We hadn't bargained
on the glass-chinned curiosity of the dead;
how day, never an outright victory,

could be undercut at 6am
by a cratered, toothless smile, hanging
low over the all-night supply.

Thus, jumping cows, astrolabes
and madness re-waxed
to the magnetic chant of king tides.

The sun, though, had taken down
more moons in its time
than it cared to count flares or ides.

It always came up fighting,
the same white-eyed bully,
the muscular surmise.

Nose low, out of joint,
it made short shrift of rematch
in silk-blue skies;

then, incredulous, saw us stake
our corner. The moon, out
for the count, wisely retired.

But we took it up to the sun,
in fightclubs of thin atmosphere;
in foolish suits of earth we flew

into its roped surprise.

Call centre

My job: to field distress calls.
To keep people on the line.
No more water trucks or airlifts.
We knew that. There were hundreds outside,
the world a giant camp, wired and waiting.
We didn't let on. There were no overt statements.
There's always hope, I'd say.
Jane, next to me on headsets, said the same.
We read off cards, points one to seven.
We had government-issue bottles.
We never spoke to the same person twice.
That was forbidden.
People had become burned by chatroom funerals —
something the last government came up with,
the talk thing. Talking cures.
Currency was old world, like global trade.

We learnt to talk the talk.
To be efficient.
The talk was always the same.
We had voice converters for language.
We had boned up on customary departure.
Thoughtful of them, I felt,
the rhetorical cultural flourish.
That was my job back then, see.

It was a good time when I think back on it.
Some days I felt priestly in jeans and t-shirt.
Despite the repetition, I never got tired of it.
I'd talk them through,
my voice somnolent, kind.

I was good at despatch. That was a fact.
They didn't use that term per se.
Outsiders, that is. Insiders
didn't like using it either.
They preferred 'departure', the ring of travel,
the myth of destination.

In the end the call centres closed.
We'd known this would happen.
I miss my work.
I miss Jane, her calm voice
reading points one to seven.
I can't remember the colour of her hair.
Red, maybe.
We made our goodbyes as if we had plans.
Now I am outside.
I forget where exactly, a borderless zone.
It might be home.
Some place like that.
I don't remember the wind and heat.
But I remember my lines.
There's always Hope, I'd say.
And a final incantation: *Go in Peace*.
I close all the windows and doors.
The silver tap drips;
when water becomes memory,
go to point seven.
I am listening now.
Waiting for the call.

II: Sore

Anti-elegies

Anti-elegy 1: Poetry

Even poetry dements in the end;
fatal attractions to dank earth
and ash albums don't fool or buy time.
Poetry always cherry-picks memory
for its own ends; yet that's a
medicated narcissism for some.
Earnest elegies are often rejected
by dogs and children. Listen to them howl.
Voting for life outside of ritual.
I'm on your side; I'm with the hounds
and the kids. I won't let elegy
make you over into a bad oil painting,
don grief's cloth pantomime.
Next time I see you walking
down the street, checking for spot fires
in unseasonal autumn heat,
light fidgeting up the shape of you
between drunken ghost gums
I will laugh and say: *the death*
of my father has not made
a poet out of me, no, not yet.

Anti-elegy 2: You are here

I read 'you are here'
on a map and think of you,
limned under tar and earth and clay,
directing slowed traffic
and weighted thought by day,
turning your face by night
to rowed council moodlights,
as to star, battery torch,
and the lingering fust
of autumn burn-offs.
You are here, constellating wonder
in light and routine and soil,
still eternally, supremely confident
in the maps and grids of the living:
cemetery map reference,
44 E 19. Row Seven.

Anti-elegy 3: First Xmas

If you must do the clanking chain
and sheet let it be pure sight gag.
The quiet wit of the dead is yours.
We expect nothing less
than theatre-restaurant ghoul.
Our task, to entreat you
to turn up late to an unwrapped
Christmas of bad bon-bon jokes and
recycled gifts. We will be waiting,
patient in sodden crepe crowns,
drinking from someone else's
warm stem glass, rare cooked animals
pressing down on First World intestines.
All of us vying to claim you, memories
competing like rich courses
which may or may not be good for you.
When it's too much ha-ha, too rich or too sad
I will bang my glass, watch
my beloved, ageing relatives
pause in confusion, clutch
tiny, fluoro-toned party whistles
in the hope they'll be first off the sinking ship.
Before they jump, I confide flippantly:
the death of my father has not made
me a joke teller,
no, not yet.

Anti-elegy 4: Spade

We thought about burying you with your old spade.
But you'd have hated that, considered it waste.
No need for a *Great Escape*, though you could
have easily whistled yourself through
to the other side like Steve.
But then, soil ended up more comfort
than you thought, a Jason Recliner for life.
How you wished the same for everyone, a leather luck.

Someone else can use the spade now, you said.
I've limed the clay mound, bedded down
the summer succulents and dug out
that brutus agapanthus on the west wall.
It's all ready. Thanks for your help.
Yeah right. Help. Take it. Go on. *Take it.*
It's yours. Hose it off after use, rub olive oil
into the handle. Don't forget. I'm resting now.
Good work. Dig deep.

Anti-elegy 5: Light and water

Even with a plain pine box,
the burial cost a bomb, authenticated
lightness a clear and quick return.
Death's a quick diet in that respect,
though the anorexic spookhouse
cheapens – neither sums you up
nor summons you. Most days
light and lightness refuse to pun.
Meanwhile daylight's broken projector
screens your old movie in fits and starts.
I guard my ticket jealously,
fighting the light to scratch
you out of faded Kodachrome.
At any moment I might catch you sweeping
leaf litter down the coppery tow paths
of late afternoon. But forget ethereals.
What ifs. You always put a plant in the earth
the moment it was given to you.
Weighted it in. Now I am putting you in,
not as swiftly as you would have liked.
You have no technique, I hear you say.
Build it up around the bole. Water it in,
pat it down. That way it will flourish.
I laugh and say: *the death of my father*
has not made a gardener of me,
no, not yet.

Front

Caring for the wounded?
he said, at 88, long-soldiered by daylight.
At first I was taken aback, summoning
fronts he'd never seen,
treeless ravines where nightingales
served rather than sang.

I'd brought my mother back
from the discount denture clinic
with its laminated pics of giant tusks,
greasy grey carpets,
jousting TVs with perfect teeth.

Afterwards we roamed the antiques market.
She on two wheels, never faster
to spot a faux fob with a mechanism
more decent than dad's shot clock;
yes, we wanted to talk.

We came back to find my father
sitting half-naked in the dark,
nappy cast off; no sentence in sight,
TV news throwing gaudy shadow plays
of wars not even his.

I pressed the green buzzer,
but no-one came to collect
the wet clothing, high priests bearing
gallon containers of soap and disinfectant
— things to be sent on during a war.

A kind orderly finally came
with fresh towels; Dad on the shower chair,
watching the cold, accusatory tiles
with all the might of the other side.
I wrapped him like a baby

until we got the temperature right,
my father stammering and wincing,
El Greco pale under fluorescent spears
but patient enough from
knowing the world hot and cold.

And calling out from room 26,
his new-toothed spouse, her voice
chiming over the newsreader's
24-hour glossolalia,
a frantic, puzzling cutaway.

We showered him and tucked
him up in powdered flannelette,
turning down the altared nightlight.
It was then that he spoke, against
the white-noised whisper of risperidone:

the wounded, out climbing trees.

Drawback

The drawback was never captured in shot,
nor my family's talent for smoke rings,
their perfectly continuous lassoos,
always the same shape
as their astonishment:
O – the slow sentence of ash.

On clear nights, memory filters
back, unlitigated.

The gearing

i.m. Tom 1925–2014 and Beatrice d. 1959

When the riding boy fell hard,
a stranger stopped, spun
the spokes still, and said:
pain is invention, just as bicycles are.
The boy learnt from this, forgetting
the metal frame's twisted smile,
the aching asphalt sea.
From that point on, he paid pain
no attention. In this way, he invented
himself, moving along the crested world
like a top-of-the-range bike.
This dedicated forgetting saw
slack chains tighten, rough gears
shift smoothly under small-boy hands
until his legs powered
all the leafless streets of Brunswick.
He knew all the houses by heart, and his:
the leaking warm odours of stew,
the whiff of radiola bakelite,
the blackbird dreaming in its concrete bath,
the nightcan man coming
up the side, quiet as slippers.
Dogs stayed quiet for a man like that.

The boy had not gotten along well with his father.
Something simple like that. That's what they said,
though they weren't experts inasmuch.
Over sagging fences, in the breath between wars,

bystanders reinvented the father's face,
alive and dead in its handsome caul.
Lagered wit, good eyes and worsted suits, other women, etc.
They forgot about the falls, coming low and sure,
his tall wife and young children jumping and ducking;
his older boy covering, then putting two suburbs' ride
between the family and gearless paternity.

Saturday nights carved his father's sloped face
into cubist bottleglass. This, his only art.
Drink poured out and over darkness' melted clockface.
The man fucked up his Australian penny brightness, but not
his son's bright coin. People wanted to be round him.
Liquor's child, that is, pure as milk and responsible
as a neat-carted milkman, filling the arteries of the city
until they were white and full and blind.

At twelve, the son became a father of four.
It was part of his job, against his mother's
violet-laundered panics and the evening's tram-tracked odds,
to convey her pillion-style to her sister's house
on Saturday nights, terraced slums closing down
and away like fists. Then to ride home
and bring the others, one by one,
hidden in the laundry baskets, rubber
tyres catching in the spiteful track.

There was the disinherited aunt welcoming them
to her slum-joy (it was hers though),
while her own unsoldiered child
(who would become the rich tax agent)
played knuckles by the cooker,
glassy-eyed, counting. Like a litter of nervy wet dogs,

they drank sugared tea from chipped saucers.
They were what their cousin did not want to become.

The rider last saw his father, sartorial
in an afternoon skinful, on Sydney Road;
with little plaiting memory of his four children,
or plum-eyed wife beating his Saturday
slatterns down the hall with a broom, or teaching
their son how to plant in clay on fly-buzzed Sundays.
By the time the son understood the truth of soil,
he had a job ferrying fruit on the back of his bike
to doctors' homes in Parkville, the grocer's best boy.

He swerved to a halt that day, fruitbox straps loosening,
oranges flying off into sun and traffic like small asteroids.
This was Sydney Road. The image of the man.
Hello Tom; hello Dad. The world raining
leeks and greens; a cooking apple big as a baby head,
spiraling into the gutter. And then the plaid back receding,
sharp tie unseen except by those it was yet to strike.

The boy left behind: a twisted wheel, a geared pain,
all the sweet broken smells.
And wages – pennies, shillings and a pound.
He had never lost anything before.
That night, he dreamt of leafy streets,
ablaze with coloured globes;
the night-can man singing loud;
his mother's smile, a lit armistice.

Scapegoat

What paddock of love produced me
as an accidental goat,
dirty wool hanging low,
red-rimmed eyes scanning the spectacular table,
as if in fear that at any moment
I might end up cousin to the mint-sprigged lamb,
gifted to sibling hunger.
I haul myself in bad dress
across unmunchable floral carpets,
take my seat and unfold
the napkin of pure white art.
It's prodigal death, not return you want
I say in my best goatish bleat.
The guests appear blank though some
had feared I'd name myself this way –
the skittish attempt to save oneself,
the short-horned grace.
Dinner is served,
the bustling kitchen is cold.
The host glares, triumphal,
yet is stupidly hesitant
with the knife.

Yellow sunhat

Do I look like a person with cancer?
you ask, smiling in your pretty sun hat.
Our skins are warm, dessicated by salt and sea.
I weigh up a careful ménage
of words: 'yes', 'no', 'cancer'.
'Yes' will make it seem more true,
'no' invite false normalcy.
Not really, I laugh, pissweak.
She gives me a long look;
I'm a Sunday painter
with no eye for gradations of blue.

Later, I try on the hat,
my hair in a tight ponytail.
Under fluorescent bathroom lights
I draw breath; the sills are crammed with meds;
I look just like a person with cancer.
I must be careful not to jinx myself,
I think, cleaning my teeth hard
in bright white light.
Decay, like love and loss,
is often negotiated
in small, tight bathrooms like this.

In the dark lounge the TV flickers
on your skull like morning sun
on a small polished planet.
When I hear you sigh, I think no,
it's more like torchlight waving
all over the place
on a hummocky road.

I sit down with you and sometimes
join in the canned laughter.
It's a funny show. Funny haha.
I'm wearing your hat,
your lovely yellow straw,
looking like a person
next to another person.

Wig library, Mornington

In the wig library I read nothing.
My job is to sort hair with you,
most of which has been worn by others.
Then, inside one recently cleaned wig, I read a label:
'Lifetime Guarantee'.
Eventually I help you find the right one,
all milk bottle cheer,
not knowing how else to be,
a feathery collaborator in disguise.
I am tactful, deft among silk-lined boxes
arranged in neat stacks, A–Z,
in cahoots with the librarian's
hushed tones and naturally greying hair,
this mother superior of hair.

When we come out the moon is hanging
low and bald in daylight.
You are a stranger to it in your wavy auburn bob.
Its angry burning cannot easily be read.
You face off like two glitzy femocrats,
magnetic to the end. You insist on driving home.

I do not go to the library again.
Another friend returns your bob.
Sometimes I imagine queues of women,
already moving in the pale, choric way of ghosts
down that same, gated sea-salt street
bleached by sunlight,
discarding pretty scarves, shoes, clothes, earth
to read the classics with authority.

These days I meet you in soft-carpeted stacks,
dream-shelved. We are students again,
soft-cheeked, big-haired, hopeful.
Other times I see you dropping books and oranges
under the suggestible street lights
of late evening.
Your old text messages
bathe my pillow in small radiant arcs,
a technological kindness
close to whispering.

You say (this is what we hear),
moving between shelves,
the 600s and the 900s,
the 200s and the 300s,
that these are our hard-combed learnings,
this strange Ephesus,
this life,
its archive of crowns
ours for the taking.

Big wig

i.m. Sharon Hill

You were no footballer. Nor a footballer's wife.
You lived in the suburbs and sometimes you read
of the proliferations of celebrity cells with a dispassionate eye.
Even so, you had your own cellular time in the sun.
You married my brother in a *Fantasy Island* ceremony on Fiji.
A dwarf sang 'Sailing' on the ukelele
as you arrived in a golf buggy,
hair blowing across your eyes like plural horizons ...
My brother, proud and plump, in ill-fitting sarong and shirt.

We had swallowed worse things than cancer's horse pills:
the jazzy optimism of recovery statistics,
talk of the glorious sunset of remission,
the onset of broccoli-tufted hair
(*our very own Jean Seberg!*)
roaring you back to life,
like a biblical wind in the garden.

You wore a wig like 99's hairdo in *Get Smart,*
triple negative concealed
under a stylishly positive thatch.
But white-coat oncology and methoxamine
didn't work with the wig,
with your new, chic goblin hairstyle.
The drugs were only stylish to a point.
You left them behind with admirable tact and gentleness.

When we looked away, your cells grew wings
and flew you too close to the sun,

which had never really cared what you looked like,
absorbed daily in flaring, heartless conceits.
Then it rolled over and turned its back,
so that the days suddenly became lightless,
faster than time. Our big familial bang,
— no mere problem of science.

At the end, the hard sun relented,
sat poised on the end of your bed in the middle of the night.
Its last kind offer: an endless chemical dawn,
your chauffeur, a morphine driver,
blurring the sounds of your children playing in the white hall.
I'll take it, you said.

Eventually we opened our eyes to the glare;
to the idea of an untimely pyre.
The whole family, afflicted by a kind of singeing —
like a perm gone badly wrong.
We seemed to sway together as one for years
in breezeless, overbright corridors,
mopping heat from your limbs as if you were a saint.
Until the day came when Mary Magdalen gestures fell hopelessly away,
the wig hidden tactfully in a drawer,
and we leant once more into strange air —
chill worlds beyond the hospital wall.
One of us, new to it, learnt how to take rings off
your cold young fingers in the morgue.

The pretty wig is in the wardrobe now
hanging limp after dial-a-blessing
from the Buddhist monk;
after we spent days turning up your favorite Shirley Bassey tracks
to impinge the morphine's dull last lapping.

Afterwards (what kind of marker is that?)
we muttered prayers for you in a no-name park,
looking around feebly, like demented aristocrats
awaiting our drivers to rescue us
from bloodless revolutions such as these.

Weeks on, your credit card purchases roll in,
sweetly, exorbitantly. The new couch; the smart yellow blinds,
designer chairs, sheets and towels
– a kind of second nesting
for those dear ones used to curling about your knees
like butter, like pure needy love.
On Thursday, a glamorous, expensive auburn wig
arrives in a post pack from Hong Kong.
I am fretting, feeding your children indiscriminately, excessively.
I know nothing of Grace's allergies. I know nothing of grace.
I cannot stop the itching.
I need to speak with you.
My brother, in the lemon-coloured kitchen, does not hear,
reading the bill in a halo of morning light
as if it is a love letter.

Quota

There were no words said,
though she hadn't used her quota.
Before silence, there was something
that could be described as
a forgetting of verbs:
give, want, help, leave, know, thank,
and then, dimming repositories of nouns:
cigarette, tablets, card, ice, cloth, photo, morphine.

Her speech, *stumm* under pressure,
moving swiftly past pleasantries,
to its natural reduction point: *archive.*
Then, years afterwards,
the evacuated space of sound,
her voice dreamt of
in cavernous, echoing halls:
great palaces of the heart,
lime-dripped caves of the unsaid.

Bad history painting

We sat close through the night,
lips set in rough, dashed strokes
like minor figures
from bad history paintings,
hands held aghast above our heads
as Herod and his army
of dead-eyed doctors swept in.
We relinquished claims on words
and over-wrought gestures,
placebos and panaceas,
mythic death-bed scenes.
We knew you would not wake
for lesser human arts.

Classes of suffering: Pink ribbon

Charity is sly and likes a race.
Peak bodies proffer ribbons
to the warrior caste, *Breast Cancer Survivors,*
but only the select don full body armour,
pink bows tied to their lance.

Televisual opps heal —
not with good oncology,
but pure confessional apotheosis.
Bless me father ...
I did not know the angels
were so competitive.

She is not the wife
of some hard-to-recall,
famous sportsman. And what about Karen?
No-one shouts tales of Sapphic oncological woe
from the rooves of media obelisks.

Ordinary folk are less fit for TV jousts —
knitting chainmail takes all their time.
Why pose, thin-faced, in heavy pancake,
for sunny breakfast news in regulation armour?
Why join the *battle*

of best survivors, upbeat knights and
pink-draped Jeanne d'Arcs?
Do not go gentle or pink.
Do not sign deals; eschew ribboned
gymkhanas, contracts that heal.

For charity's a war and likes a race.

Chemo-blonde: One in thirty-five

On the radio I heard an American woman say:
one in thirty-five husbands will shave their head in solidarity.
Mine was not one of those, but loving, oh so loving
the way he poured over catalogues,

colours and styles, names and types.
Modelled by out-of-work sitcom actors from long ago,
their half-remembered smiles, the span of my life.

Brunette, blonde, ash-blonde, Asian black, tiger-striped, strawberry
blonde, curly, straight, wavy, bouffant, French roll, pixie, feathered,
layered, Cindy, JaCinta, Raquel Welch, Jaclyn Smith, Lin-wen,
Charm, Daytona, Luxe, Bree, Nirvana, Kourtney, Fanfare, Rave.
Purchasable from Incognito, Tony of Beverly, Revlon, Foxy Silver,
Dream USA, HairDo Australia, Estetica – heat friendly, quality
human hair wigs to complement your ethnic background. From
anywhere between $500 and $1300.

He decided he'd like me dark and wavy for a change.
That it might be a real turn on,
even if my blood was chemo-blonde by then,
my kisses tasting ash.
I can be that change, I offered,
generous to the last.
Ok, let's go with that one darling.
Nirvana, wavy dark. $899.
But not Asian hair, he added.
Too heavy, too black, unreal.

One in thirty-five.

Weight

It is a kind of sleep we must learn,
seasonal as spiders, our bodies
weights no web can hold.

We watch, stupefied as we grow
elephantine, fill the house
until tired shutters are shucked

open. We drag thickened ankles from
room to room, astonished at the sentence,
the lead suits that won't be neatly hung.

In the unmown afternoons, cars park
across us, seeking tarmac. We wake
as we sleep: heavy as roads slept on.

But what if weight was our intention all along,
the deceptions of stylish elegies
traded for glad, frightful earth?

In the kitchen, the broken radio preaches
static, weight loss, instant gardens;
the spider takes up its annual position in the hall.

The riotous spring is here and the dead
are industrious, mowing grassy
underworlds, light as gravity.

III: Saw

Laverton: First star

I saw the evening star switch on
above the wasted plains of Laverton.
I ditched the car as freeway lights
swung into view, jeering violet dusk,
a drowsy-drivers-die nocturne.

I let the cars pass and slept awhile
upon the stubble. I awoke, covered by
a milk field of stars. Decisively, I extracted
an extension ladder from my purse.
My plan – to climb up and rest my cheek
against a globe of star. If I could find a way
to let the ladder fall, I'd be free at last, as cool
and undriven as dead travelling light.

I wasn't blessed with that kind of luck.
She's astronomically challenged, the dry gods
whispered as I fell. They'd have me work
a different genre, jobbing live words
instead of dead stars, as if the wasted plain
could rhyme itself to life again.

As if, the stars sang.

Stream

We fight to become
the clean stream.

But not all of us run
a rapid, know water.

That neat man
is the efficient emission;

that crying woman
the brown rain falling.

That clean-shaven boy
the fudger of figures;

that smoke-wizened fisherman
the undersized carp.

That girl in the archive
the historian of liquidity;

the baby technocrat
the streamer *sans* stream;

that dirt course
your memorial coursing.

Saw

I once saw history
do laps around itself
to escape the job
of official eye
inside the centrifuge.
We kept on drinking.

Soon people came with sticks
to stop it running and circling.
They jammed its spokes shut
so that, like a cyclist,
history hurtled over itself,
back to where it began.
That's when we started dancing.

Soft-headed, helmetless,
it crashlanded so badly,
all our dreamscapes, our facts
and gyres of feeling
shrank into a strange Babel.
No-one was able to record
what had happened.
That's when we started laughing,

the sound of fallen
sticks, our new music.

Babel[2]

Therefore is the name of it called Babel; because the Lord did there confound
the language of all the earth: and from thence did the Lord
scatter them abroad upon the face of all the earth.
Genesis 11:9 KJV

In 1982 I enrol in the language
of the vanquished: German,
taught in a modernist Ziggurat
custom made for languages
and post-war poetries of aftermath.
The windows in the rooms
were painted shut from the outset.
After classes I join my friends,
attending more to my skin
condition and new tights
than to the man sweeping
stairs, the stairwell, fluorescent
with pop song ghazals.

Twenty-five years later I return
to find commerce installed
in a late-century trade-off,
a disciplinary sacking raid.
I teach poetry in that same building,
(to well-to-do girls *gifted at language*)
when a room becomes free
between accounts and accounting.
Most days, ghost words
hiss from the aircon ducts,
explaining everything and nothing.

Someone still pays displaced
engineers on TPVs to sweep
and learn a janitor's syntax.
On Thursday, I run into a new
sweeper on the face-lifted stair,
singing Adamic rap.
Excuse me, I say, and *Sorry* …
moving through dust maps,
though Europe's coffin stands
in the hall, a cautionary furniture.
But the sweeper, half-smiling,
half-safe, ushers me through,
the lightwell's falling clouds,
sweeping history clean.

---

2 The Babel Building at the University of Melbourne was custom built after World War Two for the express purpose of teaching languages. Many of these classes were taught by European refugees.

Shrine[3]

Some distance from the great white shrine,
city goers appear blindsided by cephalagia,
fingers delicately cradling handsets to crania.
The fighters, Tunnerminnerwait and Maulboyheenner,
only differentiate this from grief or sickness
when thousands thread the city streets,
making and remaking identical Goyaesque gestures
as wrenched vocabularies of laughter, loss and symbol.

You are no slouch; you became like them long ago,
having moved here voluntarily after the great fires ceased.
You have forgotten to draw the Dandenongs' petrol blue
haze about your shoulders; your feeble memory
of fired country, gone. Thus you link in and disappear,
cradling your burning white head just like the others,
as if it were a precious thing to be carried to market.

The settler streets are new but always ancient, in the way
of being crowded with users, usurpers, lovers of usury.
High above the city, the gull's red eye reads the city
as a gridded history painting. Real scale outdoes the Great Masters
but not the dreams of the fighters, returned from the dead,

an army of fear: *Peevay, Napolean, Jack of Cape Grim,*
Tunninerpareway, Robert Smallboy, Jemmy, Timmy,
Tinney Jimmy, Robert of Ben Lomond, Bob;
strong-armed, yet not yet ready to lift
their own monuments into place.

But when Tunnerminnerwait and Maulboyheenner return,
swooping down without warning on borrowed grain-fed Pegasus,
they too are caught unawares by asphalt kerbs and curtain walls,

by the stale air, the absence of a river once known
and forded with great losses on both sides.
For a moment the famed warriors are nonplussed;
the source has been built in and built over.
The burning stations and Mornington rides
rate no plaque in the victor's museum,
the tired white pamphlets – bloodless, blank.

Slowing to a canter on a stolen horse is to admit defeat.
And so, hooves clacking *fortissimo possibile*,
they raise their guns the old way
to glass and steel, briefcase and brolly.
The makers of this hooved ordinance,
deaf to the mobile pleadings of women,
to the white kerb of history,
are swift to recognise the indivisibility of old and new,
the cringing mouths and eyes of European
history paintings they have heard about but never seen.
And then they see you, hands lifted,
cradling your burning head *en tableau*.
They have come for you, to burn down
your great white shrine and take you home.

Tunnerminnerwait and Maulboyheenner were brought to Melbourne in 1839
by the protector of Aborigines, George Robinson, to 'civilise' the Victorian
Aborigines. In late 1841, the two men and three women stole two guns and
waged a six-week guerilla-style campaign in the Dandenongs and on the
Mornington Peninsula, burning stations and killing two sealers. They were
charged with murder and tried in Melbourne. Their defence counsel was
Redmond Barry, who questioned the legal basis of British authority over
Aborigines. Thirty-nine years later, Barry would sentence Ned Kelly to hang.
Tunnerminnerwait and Maulboyheenner were the first men to be hung in
Melbourne.

Greenfield development

The white farmer takes a piece of flat earth to market. She is no flat earther.
But the land's overcropped, and she's *sotto voce* with the throb
of four generations' profit and loss. Skin cancers profit her brow,
hands, arms and legs; four sons field the catch in her voice,
fence her in so she sells quickly. Her nib bleeds out over the contract,
fine cursive streams going nowhere. Hawkish, a pair of cufflinks
and a pair of wide agate eyes, watch. Fast settlements confuse
attachment, history. *Wadawurrung. Wadawurrung.*
When did her boys begin to look like undertakers? She reaches
for her comb, hands it to her middle-aged youngest, his Adam's apple
a jitterbug combine. He wants the deal more than any of them,
is neat enough (most days) to shake hands with a city future.
Outside, the horizon squints, elongates in the heat.
The blistered ute bonnet, parked beside the agent's new car,
rebukes; yet her father's cataract stare once frightened bailiffs.
After the signing, the phone's off for days. When she sees
her best fields carved up, pink allotment flags blowing in the wind,
she thinks it's some new kind of sow stall.
Then lifestyle's cropless verbs appear as billboard signs.
O bury me under the latte lake, she thinks, looking out
her kitchen window, from a past of minute hands,
good black earth and sponges sunk in the middle.
Next day, billboards truck to the lee of the sales office, marooned in dirt.
Old ewes with pinprick eyes nudge carpeted heads in puzzlement,
gather by strange rectangles of shade. New-poured slabs,
white as snow, cramp thin soil, portals to nowhere.
She holds her mug tight, holds and breaks,
all the lambing woolly beauty of memory.

Milksop

In olden times, a child sensitive
as a reed was deemed a milksop,
milquetoast, pantywaist, pansy.
The milk supper, an attachment
to the breast, guaranteed, they said,
an eternal six-foot childhood.
One lily-livered lad, too patient for
conventional ruin, asked quietly if he
could be taught fighting and world.

The lord and bully who knocked
him down, years later in the timid yard,
wore his breeches longer than a pantywaist,
often using a knuckle-dusted punch to fight.
The sop that night was one of five bastards
he had fathered in the pretty village.
He'd teach him a lesson for existing;
he'd loved the lad's mother most.

He imagined *her* as he swung, rugged self
forgetful of what his good self might be.
But his old love shewed herself alive
in the slant gaze of the hazel-eyed boy,
and in front of such a handsome crowd!

Sending the boy's mother out upon the lake
in an uncaulked dory had worked a treat years back.
But there were nights when she rowed
into his dreams on the milk tide of memory,
against the wishes of his wife. So he swung

twice then thrice against his random
seed, blood pupils roiling, the drowned
woman crying out from the bruised seas
of her son's milky iris.

Afterwards, his underlings, nary a sop among them,
rinsed blood from the cobbled abattoir and went in
for bread, dripping and ale, looking for pleasure.

The economy of lips: Revolution

They criticised the girls
shortly after,
for putting on lipstick
the same colour
as the blood
and the banners.
It was too soon,
they said,
having only fallen
yesterday in the square.
Could painted manner
be less than manners?

But the wasp-waisted boys
in their blazers, blazing,
understood and shrieked:
There *is* a need for colour!
After a dictator has toppled,
there *is* a need for colour!'
But who heard the ancient
megaphone blur and falter?
Who saw pale economies
carried out
on long, clean stretchers?
How dull the doctor's voice, and even duller.

After the hospital
they were mostly quiet,
the young men,
going home,
in thrall to the mint-green peace

of anaesthetic.
By the service roads,
the girls waited
with food and bandages and songs,
mouthing red notes,
while frightened fathers
waited by the gate,
lipless, apologetic.

Pilgrims

know all roads lead to Rome;
the rouged glass mouth
of a window rose
told them so. Oh,
how beautiful it was,
crystal colours: hope, love, charity —
the afterimage of being touched.
Jesus, the smell of cheap hotels!
His canonical grip
on the steering wheel,
her hands fluttering
over digital maps, a looser faith.
They drive five countries wide
for one papal wave, lunch
with true believers.
Outside the city, they pause
on gilt-edged roads for tea
and museums. They are out of sugar,
but they know the first signs
of a marble headache,
Raphael's high-key clouds
a cyclamate pageant,
a sweetness they cannot access.
The weary colonnades expect them,
St Peter surly on the pediment.
Don't be late, friends! There!
Pinkie rising plump and expectant,
a beringed hand high above
a holy sea of men and women,
pockets full of secreted condoms
and Vatican City stamps.

She exits the car before he can pull up.
The Ascension Giftshop's
a good place to park, she says,
not looking back,
running towards love.

Acknowledgements

Epigraphs for this book are extracted from 'A war in the air' by Howard Nemerov, *in The Collected Poems of Howard Nemerov* (The University of Chicago Press, 1977); and 'My grandmother's grave' by Dunya Mikhail, in *Poetry* magazine (December 2014).

Versions of the following poems found publication in a range of journals and broadsheets, and I thank the editors of these publications for these opportunities.

'Love song' appeared in *The Age*. 'Soar', 'Big wig' and 'Weight' were published in issues of *Australian Book Review*, with 'Soar' republished in *The Best Australian Poems 2013*. 'Classes of suffering', 'One in thirty-five', 'Drawback', 'Yellow sunhat', 'Bad history painting' and 'Quota' were published in *Now You Shall Know: Newcastle Poetry Prize Anthology 2013*. 'Wig library' was published in *A Sudden Presence: Poetry from the Inaugural ACU Literature Prize 2013*. 'Shrine' appeared in *Dazzled: The University of Canberra Vice-Chancellor's International Poetry Prize 2014*. 'The economy of lips: Revolution' and 'Front' were published in *The Language of Compassion: Poetry from the Second ACU Literature Prize*. 'Anti-elegies' was published in *Australian Book Review* (States of Poetry 2016) and subsequently in *The Best Australian Poems 2016*. 'Greenfield development' was published in *The Canberra Times* in 2016 and *The Best Australian Poems 2017*. 'The gearing' was published in *Island* in 2017.

I want to thank publisher David Musgrave and Ann Vickery at Puncher and Wattmann for helping make this book. I thank anyone held captive by rough drafts, especially Anthony Lynch, my best reader, supporter and sounding board. Special thanks to David McCooey and Lisa Gorton for additional kind encouragement in recent years through the publication of individual poems. I am grateful to Kevin Brophy and Maria Takolander for their wordsmithery. The poetry students I teach at the University of Melbourne have inspired me along the way, as have Gracie and Charlie Johnson, who sometimes read poems with me, especially animal poems.

I also want to mark the support of my late father, Tom Johnson, to whom this book is dedicated.

A. Frances Johnson

Biographical Note

A. Frances Johnson is a prize-winning poet, author and artist, and a senior lecturer in Creative Writing at the University of Melbourne. *Rendition for Harp & Kalashnikov* is her third book of poetry. In 2012, her collection *The Wind-up Birdman of Moorabool Street* (Puncher and Wattmann) won the Wesley Michel Wright Prize. In 2015, she won the Griffith University Josephine Ulrick Poetry Prize. She was also the 2017 recipient of the Australia Council writing residency to the B.R. Whiting Studio in Rome.

www.ingramcontent.com/pod-product-compliance
Lightning Source LLC
Chambersburg PA
CBHW031003090426
42737CB00008B/662